My Day **with the Cup**

SIDNEY CROSBY

PHOTOGRAPHY | BRAD MCCAUGHAN

FENN
Fenn Publishing Company Ltd.

We would like to thank the Canadian Armed Forces and the Hockey Hall of Fame for thier support
and contribution to this celebration with the Stanley Cup

PHOTO CREDITS:
Photography by Brad McCaughan with the following exceptions

Page 3 young Sidney Crosby—courtesy Crosby family

Pages 5 to 16 Military event—photos courtesy Department National Defence

Pages 25 & 26 IWK visit—photos by Mike Dembeck

Page 59 Sidney with RCMP officer—photo by Mike Dembeck

Page 61 Sidney receiving cup from Philip Pritchard—photo Mike Dembeck

Page 74 photo courtesy Nova Scotia Sport Hall of Fame

Page 75 Sidney with Cup on dryer—photo by Philip Pritchard / HHOF

Page 78 1st day of school—courtesy Crosby family

Page 83 Walt Neubrand and Brad McCaughan—photo Carolyn McCaughan

It was better than I ever could have imagined.

I got to live out two childhood dreams in one year—winning the Stanley Cup, and bringing it back to my hometown of Cole Harbour, Nova Scotia. I was able to share it with my family, my friends, and so many people who have supported me for so long, in many different ways. My goal was to do as much as possible and share the experience with as many people as I could during my two days. Looking back, it could not have been more perfect. The weather was great, the reaction was phenomenal—and the best part was being able to see so many people celebrating together.

The Stanley Cup travels around the world and commands admiration and attention wherever it goes. That's because it is the symbol of a champion. It represents the work of a group of people who achieved a common goal through sacrifice, plain hard work, and by overcoming adversity.

For those who experienced the Cup coming to Cole Harbour, I hope this book acts as a great reminder of that unique celebration. For those who were not able to make it, well, maybe this can be your way of experiencing it, of feeling what we all felt during those two special days.

I am very fortunate to be able to share these tremendous memories—and I hope this is just the start. My dream is to spend many days and create many more memories with hockey's holy grail. And, hopefully, we can all celebrate together again.

ST. JOHN'S

ZULU

MADRID

8:32 am Waiting for the Cup

8:52 am Phil Pritchard / HHOF delivers the Stanley Cup

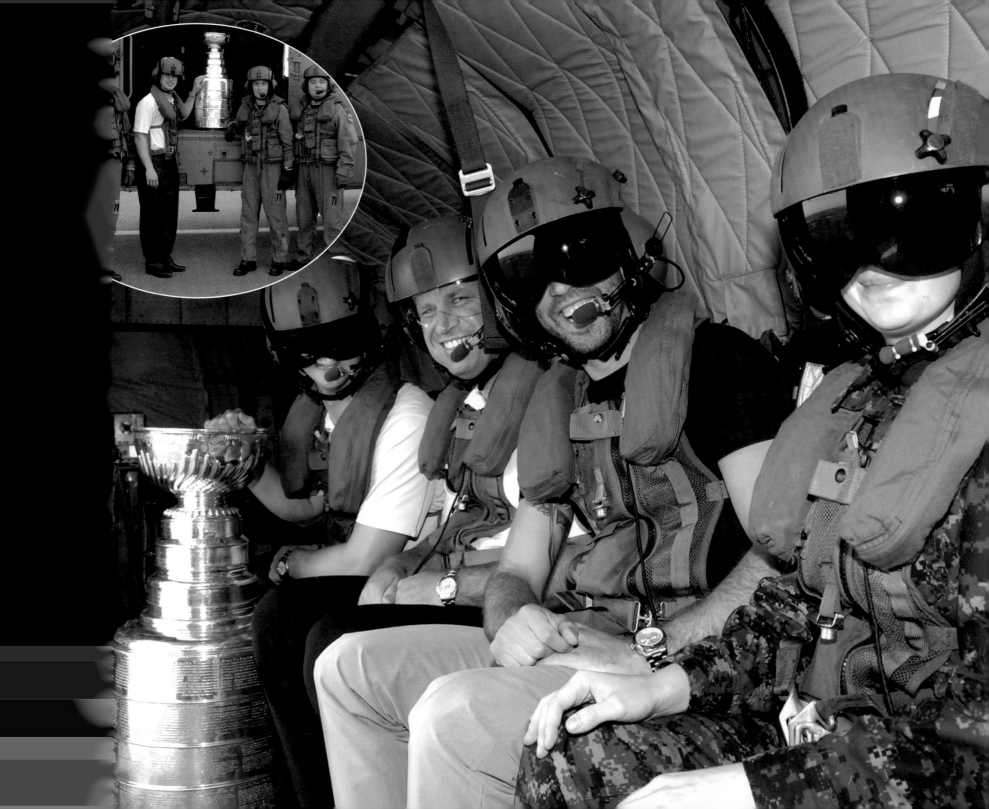

9:03 am On-board Sea King helicopter

9:29 am Arrive at HMC Dockyard, CFB Halifax, Nova Scotia

9:34 am With Rear Admiral Paul Maddison & Right Honourable Peter MacKay

9:42 am Maxime Talbot with Prince of Wales Trophy; me with Stanley Cup

9:48 am Reception aboard the HMC *Preserver*

9:56 am Meeting the press

 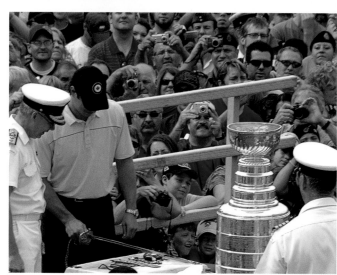 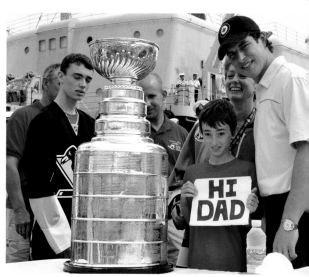
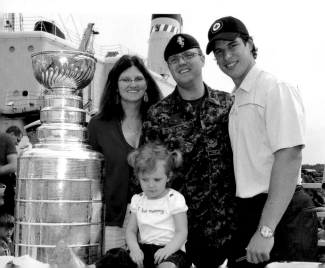  

10:43 am My first time in an armoured personnel carrier with the Cup

Citadel Hill is one of the places where I train in the summers.

While running the hill, I would often think of the Stanley Cup—winning it has always been my goal, and it motivated me. So to be able to bring the Cup to Citadel Hill was a very special experience. From the top of the hill, you can see the whole city of Halifax, from the town clock, across to Dartmouth and the oil refinery. I always make sure I take in the sights, rain or shine. This is very much a part of me. And now I'll be even more motivated when I train here in the future.

11:26 am In front of Halifax Metro Centre where Max and I both won the QMJHL President's Cup

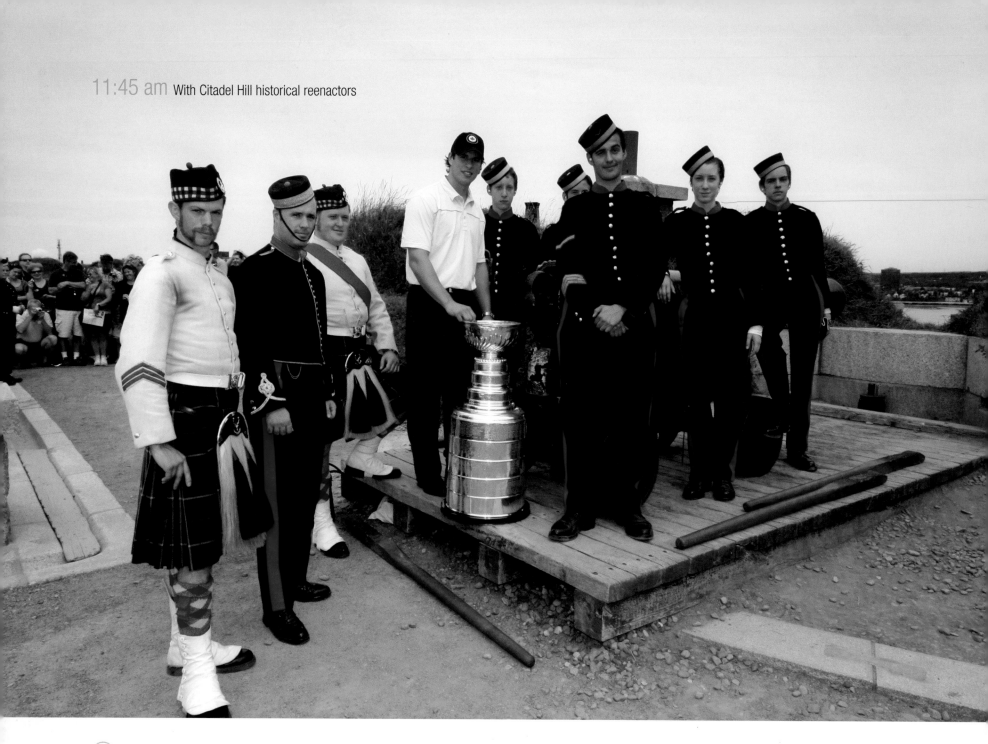

11:45 am With Citadel Hill historical reenactors

12:00 pm I gave the command to fire the 12-noon cannon

12:03 pm Bagpiper plays me "Happy Birthday"

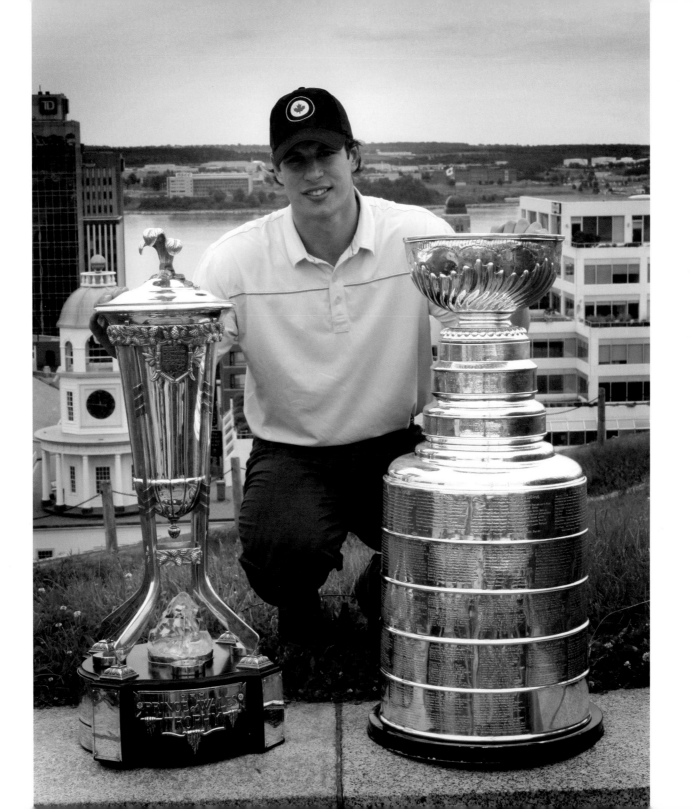

Happy Birthday

WELCOME SIDNEY!

87

87

12:33 pm Visiting kids at IWK Children's Hospital

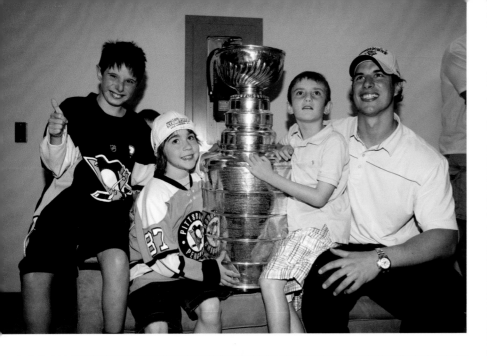

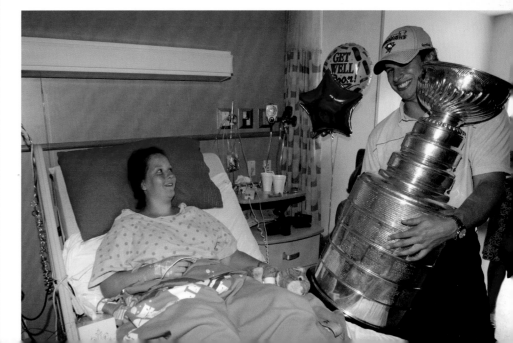

2:19 pm Getting ready for the parade

2:22 pm I was made an honourary member of the Halifax DND fire department by Ron LeRue

Congratulations Sidney from your friends at Tim Hortons

2:28 pm With the Timbit hockey players who would ride in the parade

2:32 pm Halifax Regional Municipality police motorcade

2:35 pm The parade begins

2:38 pm Military band

Nanny Crosby
& Nanny Forbes

2:40 pm My grandmothers: Nanny Crosby and Nanny Forbes

2:42 pm The gang from Q 104, a local radio station

2:43 pm Max Talbot with the Prince of Wales Trophy

Maxime Talbot

MacPhee
PONTIAC

ESSO

POLICE

TALBOT
25

D-18928

2:44 pm Cole Harbour Road

3:14 pm Waiting to get into Cole Harbour Place, my old hockey rink

In travelling with the Stanley Cup since 1988

it became obvious to me pretty quickly that these couple of days were going to be special. There was a buzz in the air as we landed at the Halifax airport early on August 7. It was already in the papers, people were talking about it, the pilot was talking about it…and we had barely hit the ground. It wasn't even 8:00 a.m.

Everything went smoothly, and Sidney (like a true champion) made sure nobody was left behind. From the ride in the helicopter, to meeting the Armed Forces, everything was first class. As Walter and I walked beside the fire truck during the parade, you could see how much Cole Harbour meant to Sidney and how much Sidney meant to Cole Harbour. People drove for miles to be part of one of Cole Harbour's biggest events. Signs were made welcoming him home, wishing him happy birthday. It was amazing to see how many people shared the same birthday as him. It truly was a great homecoming for a great human being who will never forget his roots.

Those two days rank up there as some of the most unique travels the Stanley Cup has had. They couldn't have happened without Sidney, his family and his extended family—the people from Cole Harbour."

—Philip Pritchard / HHOF

3:27 pm Waiting backstage

3:50 pm Receiving awards from MP Mike Savage and Mayor Peter Kelly

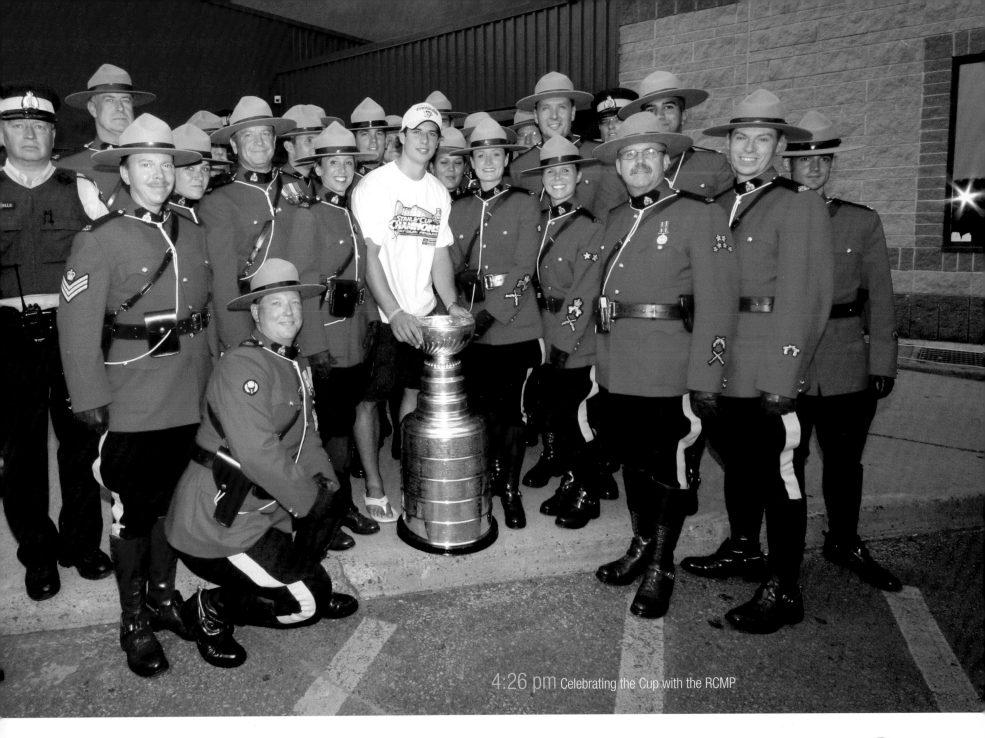

4:26 pm Celebrating the Cup with the RCMP

4:29 pm Timbits 3-on-3 hockey

5:15 pm Onstage with Max for a hot-stove session with the fans.

Whenever I allowed myself

to imagine bringing the Stanley Cup home to Cole Harbour, I always envisioned playing ground hockey with my buddies. It seemed like the obvious thing to do. Ever since we were six or seven years old, we had played so many games on the street, lake or pond, competing for the "Cup"—but never the real one. Now, I had the chance to play a game with those same guys, and the real Stanley Cup was our prize. And, win or lose, everyone got to hold it.

6:11 pm Outdoor ground-hockey game

Celebrating the Cup with friends (back row: John Chiasson, Mike Chiasson, Jeff Kielbratowski, Nathan Welton, Sidney Crosby, Matt Foston, Scott Leverman, (front) Corey Banfield, Andrew Newton)

7:52 pm Sam Roberts Band onstage at Cole Harbour Place

8:24 pm Thanking my fans

9:03 pm Dartmouth waterfront

9:50 pm Showing the Cup to crowds watching the Halifax International Buskers Festival

10:12 pm Raising the Stanley Cup for the tall ship *Silva*

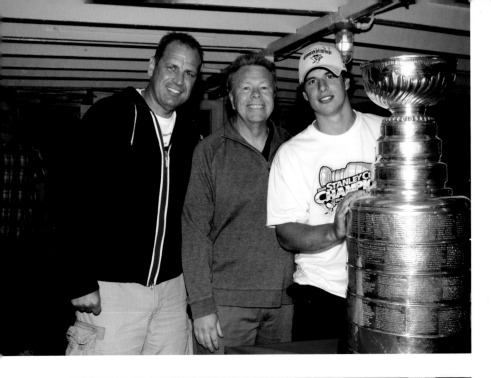

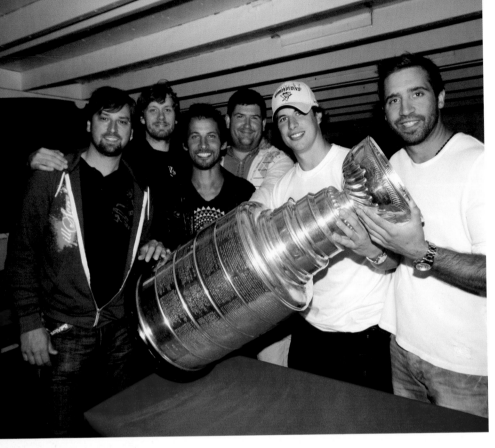
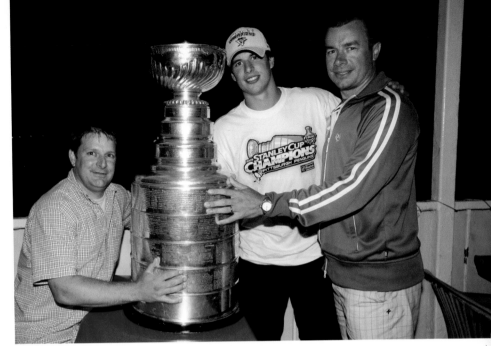

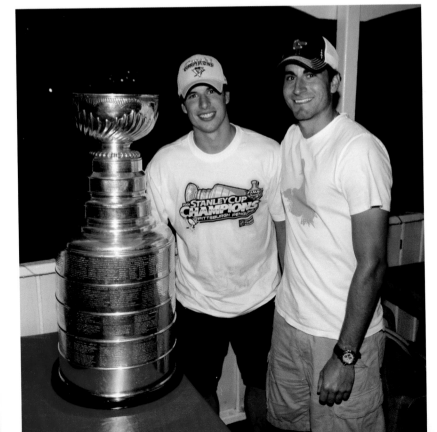

HARBOUR QUEEN I

HARBOUR TOURS
DINNER CRUISES
PARTY CRUISES
420-1015
www.murphysonthewater.com

10:30 pm Leaving the *Harbour Queen*

10:50 pm Downtown Halifax

71

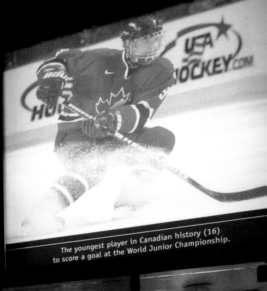

The youngest player in Canadian history (16) to score a goal at the World Junior Championship.

At the Nova Scotia Sport Hall of Fame with my agent Pat Brisson and his family, along with the Stanley Cup and my mom's puck-marked dryer

The Nova Scotia Sport Hall of Fame would like to congratulate Sidney for bringing the Cup home to Nova Scotia and inspiring the youth in our province to become Nova Scotia Sport Heroes

DREAMS

REALITY

Come visit the Sidney Crosby Exhibit at the Nova Scotia Sport Hall of Fame
HALIFAX METRO CENTRE

9:45 am My mom's puck-marked dryer

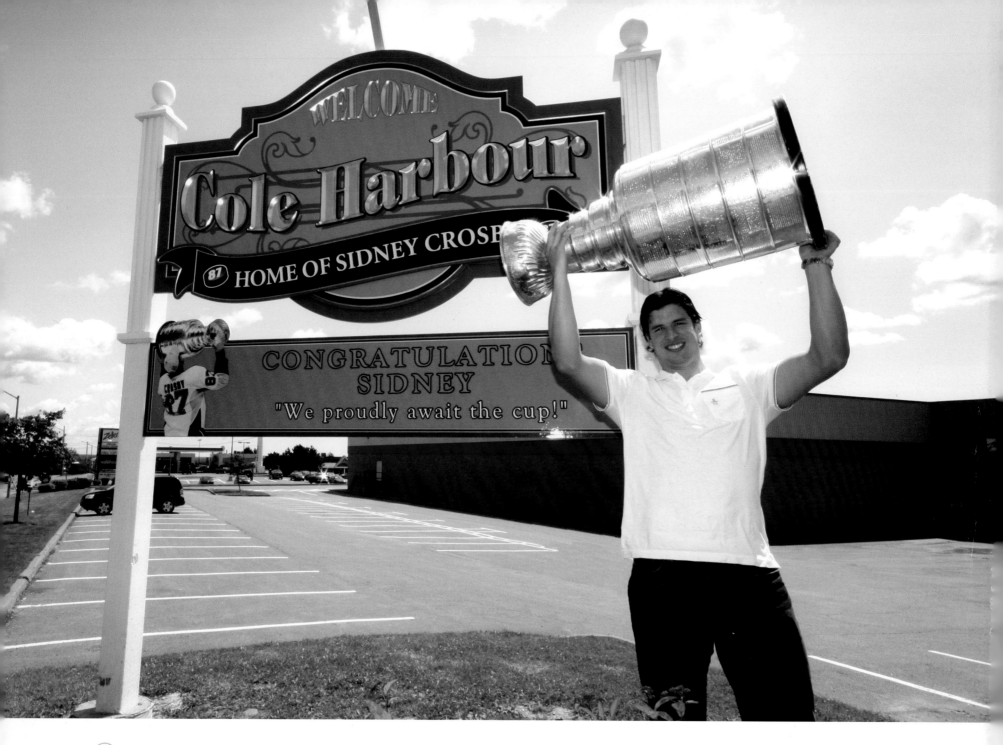

Sept 1992 Me looking at my dad on my first day of school

COLONEL JOHN STUART ELEMENTARY SCHOOL

Seventeen years later

ALL VISITORS
RT TO
FICE

With my sister, Taylor

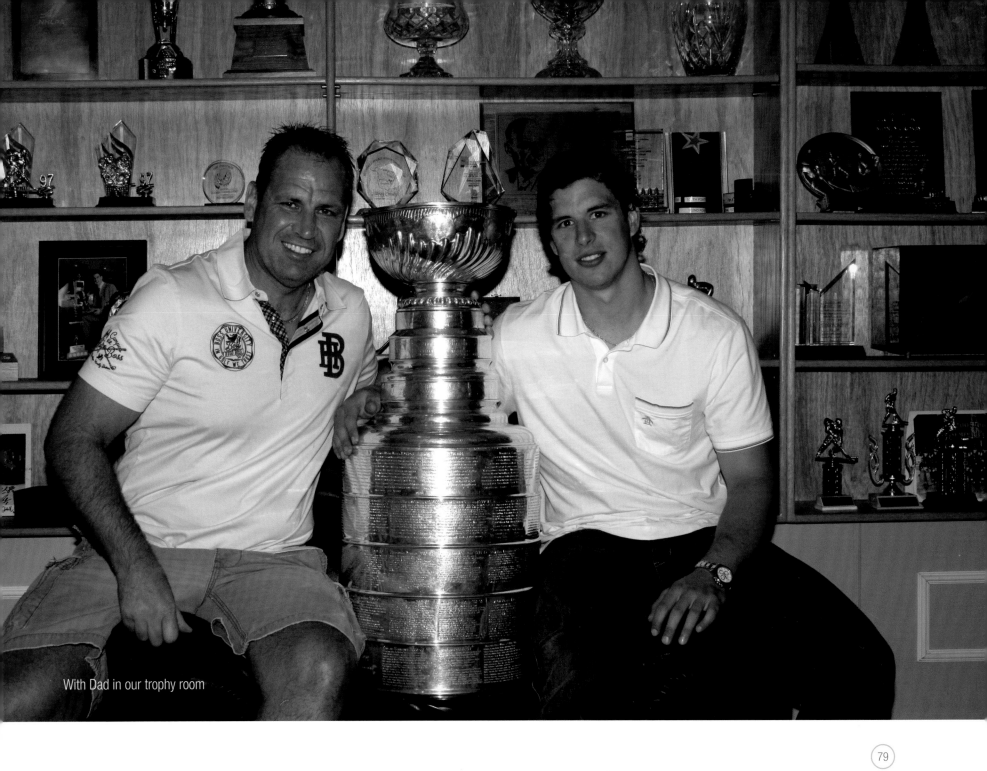

With Dad in our trophy room

Enjoying our backyard deck

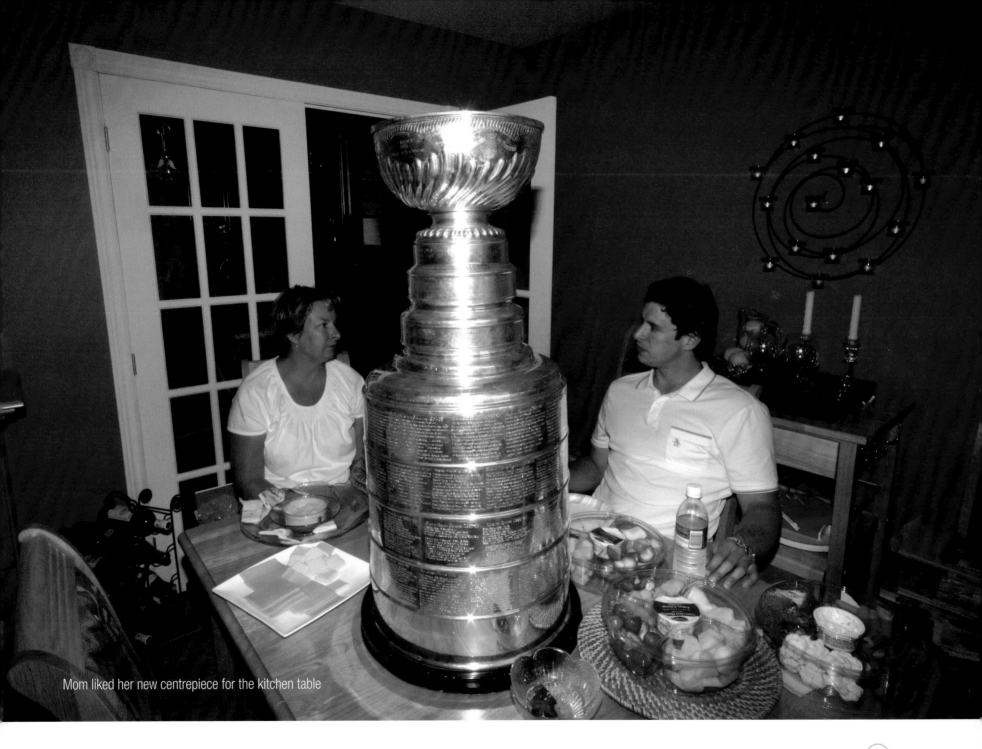

Mom liked her new centrepiece for the kitchen table

Cleaning the Cup

An interesting and helpful part of Sidney's day was his offering to clean the Cup for us. It caught us off guard, but after he explained it, it made perfect sense. He wanted to experience the Cup at all levels, and this was one aspect of doing that. Great! Very few players ever think of that.

I informed Sidney that he needed some liquid dishwashing soap, a small hand towel, a regular towel and a garden hose. Once all these things were obtained, off he went. We use these items to clean the Cup because silver polish, if used consistently, will take the finish off the Cup. And we usually don't have the time for silver polish as it takes about an hour to do. We've cleaned the Cup in backyards, hotel rooms and even airport washrooms!

Sid began with the bowl. He poured the soap in and started scrubbing. It was a different approach as we usually put the soap in and blast it with water to have it overflow with foam, but Sidney's way worked. As long as it's clean, right?

Sidney showed he is a rookie at some things when he questioned whether he should clean the rest of the Cup. "Uh…yes. It's not 1893, there is a lot more than just the bowl." Sidney promptly washed the rest of the Cup, dried it, and did an excellent job. He proudly brought it out for his guests for many, many more pictures and good times. We didn't have to clean it for the rest of the night!

—Walter Neubrand / HHOF

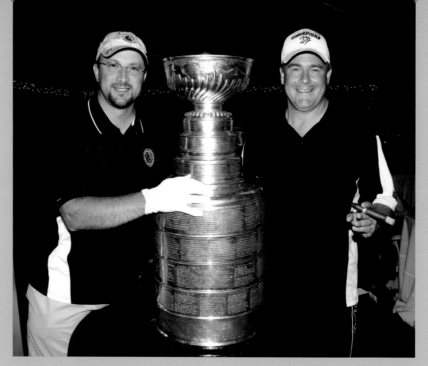

Walter Neubrand and Brad McCaughan

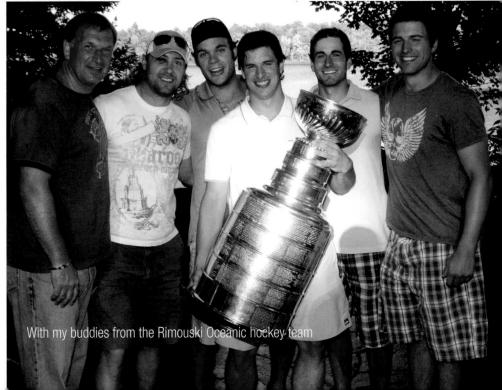

With my buddies from the Rimouski Oceanic hockey team

Acknowledgements

All the preparation for this one amazing day began the day after the Stanley Cup win, with one phone call from my mom and dad to Paul Mason—a family friend in Cole Harbour. What followed were hours, days and weeks of preparation.

To all to the organizations, people and places we visited that day—the Canadian military, the IWK Health Centre, the folks at Citadel Hill—thank you for your time and commitment! I was so proud to make each one of you part of my day with the Cup.

For all of the volunteers who sacrificed actually seeing and taking part in the festivities at Cole Harbour Place—many from my very own Cole Harbour Minor Hockey Association—thank you. This day would not have happened without you. From setting up the day before, to selling hotdogs and hamburgers, to organizing and selling posters and T-shirts, to working games and other activities—we had volunteers for everything. And then there was clean up! For all of this and to all of you, I am sincerely thankful for your hard work in making my day—our day—in Cole Harbour a very special one!

Being able to celebrate the Stanley Cup on my birthday with my family and friends just made the whole experience that much better. I want to recognize Phil Pritchard and Walter Neubrand from the Hockey Hall of Fame for making that possible.

I want to thank Brad McCaughan for all the wonderful photos he took that day—they will help me and others relive the day for years to come.

And finally, to my friends at CAA Sports, for all their hard work in making this book happen.

Fenn Publishing Company Ltd.

My Day with the Cup
A Fenn Publishing Book / First Published in 2009

Library and Archives Canada Cataloguing in Publication data available upon request

ONTARIO ARTS COUNCIL
CONSEIL DES ARTS DE L'ONTARIO

THE CANADA COUNCIL | LE CONSEIL DES ARTS
FOR THE ARTS | DU CANADA
SINCE 1957 | DEPUIS 1957

The publisher gratefully acknowledges the support of the Canada Council for the Arts and the Ontario Arts Council
for its publishing program. We acknowledge the support of the Government of Ontario through the Ontario Media
Development Corporation's Ontario Book Initiative.

We acknowledge the financial support of the Government of Canada through the Book Publishing Industry
Development Program (BPIDP) for our publishing activities.

Care has been taken to trace ownership of copyright material in this book and to secure permissions. The
publishers will gladly receive any information that will enable them to rectify errors or omissions.

Designed by Sonya V. Thursby—opushouse.ca—based on Jacques Gaudet's initial work.

Fenn Publishing Company Ltd.
Toronto, Ontario, Canada

Mixed Sources
Cert no. SW-COC-001271
© 1996 FSC

FSC

Printed and bound in Canada

09 10 11 12 13 5 4 3 2 1